let's cook

baking

Emma
Patmore

p

Contents

Sticky Chocolate Pudding

These individual puddings always look impressive at the end of a meal.

Serves 6

INGREDIENTS

125 g/4¹/₂ oz/¹/₂ cup butter, softened
150 g/5¹/₂ oz/³/₄ cup soft
   brown sugar
3 eggs, beaten
pinch of salt
25 g/1 oz cocoa powder

125 g/4¹/₂ oz/1 cup self-raising flour
25 g/1 oz dark chocolate,
   chopped finely
75 g/2³/₄ oz white chocolate,
   chopped finely

SAUCE:
150 ml/5 fl oz/²/₃ cup double
   (heavy) cream
75 g/2³/₄ oz/¹/₃ cup soft brown sugar
25 g/1 oz/6 tsp butter

1 Lightly grease 6 individual 175 ml/6 fl oz/³/₄ cup pudding basins (molds).

2 In a bowl, cream together the butter and sugar until pale and fluffy. Beat in the eggs a little at a time, beating well after each addition.

3 Sieve (strain) the salt, cocoa powder and flour into the creamed mixture and fold through the mixture. Stir the chopped chocolate into the mixture until evenly combined.

4 Divide the mixture between the prepared pudding basins (molds). Lightly grease 6 squares of foil and use them to cover the tops of the basins (molds). Press around the edges to seal.

5 Place the basins (molds) in a roasting tin (pan) and pour in boiling water to come halfway up the sides of the basins (molds).

6 Bake in a preheated oven, 180°/350°F/Gas Mark 4, for 50 minutes, or until a skewer inserted into the centre comes out clean.

7 Remove the basins (molds) from the roasting tin (pan) and set aside while you prepare the sauce.

8 To make the sauce, put the cream, sugar and butter into a pan and bring to the boil over a gentle heat. Simmer gently until the sugar has dissolved.

9 To serve, run a knife around the edge of each pudding, then turn out on to serving plates. Pour the sauce over the top of the puddings and serve immediately.

Chocolate Brownie Roulade

The addition of nuts and raisins has given this dessert extra texture,
making it similar to that of chocolate brownies.

Serves 8

INGREDIENTS

150 g/5^1/$_2$ oz dark chocolate, broken
into pieces
3 tbsp water
175 g/6 oz/^{3}/$_4$ cup caster
(superfine) sugar

5 eggs, separated
25 g/1 oz/2 tbsp raisins, chopped
25 g/1 oz pecan nuts, chopped
pinch of salt

300 ml/^{1}/$_2$ pint/1^1/$_4$ cups double
(heavy) cream, whipped lightly
icing (confectioners') sugar, for
dusting

1 Grease a 30 x 20 cm/12 x 8
inch swiss roll tin (pan), line
with baking parchment and grease
the parchment.

2 Melt the chocolate with the
water in a small saucepan
over a low heat until the chocolate
has just melted. Leave to cool.

3 In a bowl, whisk the sugar
and egg yolks for 2-3 minutes
with a hand-held electric whisk
until thick and pale.

4 Fold in the cooled chocolate,
raisins and pecan nuts.

5 In a separate bowl, whisk the
egg whites with the salt. Fold
one quarter of the egg whites into
the chocolate mixture, then fold
in the rest of the whites, working
lightly and quickly.

6 Transfer the mixture to the
prepared tin (pan) and bake in
a preheated oven, 180°C/350°F/
Gas Mark 4, for 25 minutes until
risen and just firm to the touch.
Leave to cool before covering with
a sheet of non-stick baking
parchment and a damp clean tea
towel (dish cloth). Leave until
completely cold.

7 Turn the roulade out on to
another piece of baking
parchment dusted with icing
(confectioner's) sugar and remove
the lining paper.

8 Spread the cream over the
roulade. Starting from a short
end, roll the sponge away from
you using the paper to guide you.
Trim the ends of the roulade to
make a neat finish and transfer to a
serving plate. Leave to chill in the
refrigerator until ready to serve.
Dust with a little icing
(confectioners') sugar before
serving, if wished.

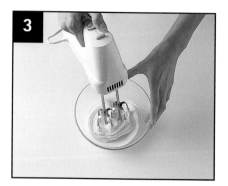

Orange Tart

*This is a variation of the classic lemon tart – in this recipe
fresh breadcrumbs are used to create a thicker texture.*

Serves 6-8

INGREDIENTS

PASTRY (PIE DOUGH):
150 g/5 oz/1¼ cups plain (all-
  purpose) flour
25 g/1 oz/5 tsp caster (superfine)
  sugar
125 g /4½ oz/½ cup butter, cut
  into small pieces

1 tbsp water

FILLING:
grated rind of 2 oranges
9 tbsp orange juice
50 g/1¾ oz/⅞ cups fresh white
  breadcrumbs

2 tbsp lemon juice
150 ml/¼ pint/⅔ cup single
  (light) cream
50 g/1¾ oz/¼ cup butter
50 g/1¾ oz/¼ cup caster
  (superfine) sugar
2 eggs, separated
pinch of salt

1 To make the pastry (pie dough), place the flour and sugar in a bowl and rub in the butter with your fingers. Add the cold water and work the mixture together until a soft pastry (pie dough)has formed. Wrap and leave to chill for 30 minutes.

2 Roll out the dough and line a 24 cm/9½ inch loose-bottomed quiche/flan tin (pan). Prick the pastry (pie dough) with a fork and leave to chill for 30 minutes.

3 Line the pastry case (pie shell) with foil and baking beans and bake in a preheated oven, 190°C/375°F/ Gas Mark 5, for 15 minutes. Remove the foil and beans and cook for 15 minutes.

4 To make the filling, mix the orange rind and juice and the breadcrumbs in a bowl. Stir in the lemon juice and single (light) cream. Melt the butter and sugar in a pan over a low heat. Remove the pan from the heat, add the

2 egg yolks, the salt and the breadcrumb mixture and stir.

5 In a mixing bowl, whisk the egg whites with a pinch of salt until they form soft peaks. Fold them into the egg yolk mixture.

6 Pour the filling mixture into the pastry case (pie shell). Bake in a preheated oven, 170°C/ 325°F/Gas Mark 3, for about 45 minutes or until just set. Leave to cool slightly and serve warm.

Apricot & Cranberry Frangipane Tart

This tart is ideal to make at Christmas time when fresh cranberries are in abundance.
If liked, brush the warm tart with 2 tbsp melted apricot jam.

Serves 8–10

INGREDIENTS

PASTRY (PIE DOUGH):
150 g/5^1/2 oz/1^1/4 cups plain (all-purpose) flour
125 g/4^1/2 oz/^{1}/2 cup caster (superfine) sugar
125 g/4^1/2 oz/^{1}/2 cup butter, cut into small pieces
1 tbsp water

FILLING:
200 g/7 oz/1 cup unsalted butter
200g/7 oz/1 cup caster (superfine) sugar
1 egg
2 egg yolks
40 g/1^1/2 oz/6 tbsp plain (all-purpose) flour, sieved (strained)

175 g/6 oz/1^2/3 cups ground almonds
4 tbsp double (heavy) cream
411 g/14^1/2 oz can apricot halves, drained
125 g/4^1/2 oz fresh cranberries

1 To make the pastry (pie dough), place the flour and sugar in a bowl and rub in the butter with your fingers. Add the water and work the mixture together until a soft pastry (pie dough) has formed. Wrap and leave to chill for 30 minutes.

2 On a lightly floured surface, roll out the dough and line a 24 cm/9^1/2 inch loose-bottomed quiche/flan tin (pan). Prick the pastry (pie dough) with a fork and leave to chill for 30 minutes.

3 Line the pastry case (pie shell) with foil and baking beans and bake in a preheated oven, 190°C/375°F/Gas Mark 5, for 15 minutes. Remove the foil and baking beans and cook for a further 10 minutes.

4 To make the filling, cream together the butter and sugar until light and fluffy. Beat in the egg and egg yolks, then stir in the flour, almonds, and cream.

5 Place the apricot halves and cranberries on the bottom of the pastry case (pie shell) and spoon the filling over the top.

6 Bake in the oven for about 1 hour, or until the topping is just set. Leave to cool slightly, then serve warm or cold.

White Chocolate & Almond Tart

*This is a variation on the classic pecan pie recipe – here nuts
and chocolate are encased in a thick syrup filling.*

Serves 8

INGREDIENTS

PASTRY (PIE DOUGH):
150 g/5 oz/1^{1}/$_{4}$ cups plain (all-
    purpose) flour
25 g/1 oz/5 tsp caster (superfine)
    sugar
125 g/4^{1}/$_{2}$ oz/^{1}/$_{2}$ cup butter, cut
    into small pieces

1 tbsp water

FILLING:
150 g/5^{1}/$_{2}$ oz/^{1}/$_{2}$ cup golden
    (light corn) syrup
50 g/1^{3}/$_{4}$ oz/10 tsp butter
75 g/2^{3}/$_{4}$ oz/^{1}/$_{3}$ cup soft brown sugar

3 eggs, lightly beaten
100 g/3^{1}/$_{2}$ oz/^{1}/$_{2}$ cup whole blanched
    almonds, roughly chopped
100 g/3^{1}/$_{2}$ oz white chocolate,
    chopped roughly
cream, to serve (optional)

1 To make the pastry (pie
shell), place the flour and
sugar in a mixing bowl and rub in
the butter with your fingers. Add
the water and work the mixture
together until a soft pastry (pie
dough) has formed. Wrap and
leave to chill for 30 minutes.

2 On a lightly floured surface,
roll out the dough and line a
24 cm/9½ inch loose-bottomed
quiche/flan tin (pan). Prick the
pastry (pie dough) with a fork and
leave to chill for 30 minutes. Line
the pastry case (pie shell) with foil
and baking beans and bake in a
preheated oven, 190°C/375°F/ Gas
Mark 5, for 15 minutes. Remove
the foil and baking beans and cook
for a further 15 minutes.

3 To make the filling, gently
melt the syrup, butter and
sugar together in a saucepan.
Remove from the heat and leave
to cool slightly. Stir in the beaten
eggs, almonds and chocolate.

4 Pour the chocolate and nut
filling into the prepared pastry
case (pie shell) and cook in the
oven for 30-35 minutes or until
just set. Leave to cool before
removing the tart from the tin
(pan). Serve with cream, if wished.

VARIATION

*You can use a mixture of white and
dark chocolate for this tart, if
preferred.*

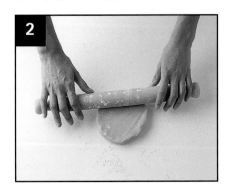

Pear Tarts

These tarts are made with ready-made puff pastry (pie dough) which is available from most supermarkets. The finished pastry is rich and buttery.

Makes 6

INGREDIENTS

250 g/9 oz fresh ready-made
   puff pastry
25 g/1 oz/8 tsp soft brown sugar

25 g/1 oz/6 tsp butter (plus extra
   for brushing)
1 tbsp stem (candied) ginger, finely
   chopped

3 pears, peeled, halved and cored
cream, to serve

1 On a lightly floured surface, roll out the pastry (pie dough). Cut out six 10 cm/4 inch round circles.

2 Place the circles on to a large baking tray (cookie sheet) and leave to chill for 30 minutes.

3 Cream together the brown sugar and butter in a small bowl, then stir in the chopped stem (candied) ginger.

4 Prick the pastry circles with a fork and spread a little of the ginger mixture on to each one.

5 Slice the pears halves lengthways, keeping the pears intact at the tip. Fan out the slices slightly.

6 Place a fanned-out pear half on top of each pastry (pie dough) circle. Make small flutes around the edge of the pastry (pie dough) circles and brush each pear half with melted butter.

7 Bake in a preheated oven, 200°C/400°F/Gas Mark 6, for 15-20 minutes until the pastry is well risen and golden. Serve warm with a little cream.

COOK'S TIP

If you prefer, serve these tarts with vanilla ice cream for a delicious dessert.

Crunchy Fruit Cake

The polenta (cornmeal) adds texture to this fruit cake, as well as an interesting golden yellow colour. It also acts as a flour, binding the ingredients together to create a lighter texture.

Serves 8–10

INGREDIENTS

100 g/3$^{1}/_{2}$ oz/$^{1}/_{3}$ cup butter, softened
100g/3$^{1}/_{2}$ oz/$^{1}/_{2}$ cup caster (superfine) sugar
2 eggs, beaten

50 g/1$^{3}/_{4}$ oz/$^{1}/_{3}$ cup self-raising flour, sieved (strained)
100 g/3$^{1}/_{2}$ oz/$^{2}/_{3}$ cup polenta (cornmeal)
1 tsp baking powder

225 g/8 oz mixed dried fruit
25 g/ 1oz pine kernels (nuts)
grated rind of 1 lemon
4 tbsp lemon juice
2 tbsp milk

1 Grease an 18 cm/7 inch cake tin (pan) and line the base with baking parchment.

2 In a bowl, whisk together the butter and sugar until light and fluffy.

3 Whisk in the beaten eggs a little at a time, whisking well after each addition.

4 Fold the flour, baking powder and polenta (cornmeal) into the mixture until well blended.

5 Stir in the mixed dried fruit, pine kernels (nuts), grated lemon rind, lemon juice and milk.

6 Spoon the mixture into the prepared tin (pan) and level the surface.

7 Bake in a preheated oven, 180°C/350°F/Gas Mark 4, for about 1 hour or until a fine skewer inserted into the centre of the cake comes out clean.

8 Leave the cake to cool in the tin (pan) before turning out.

VARIATION

To give a more crumbly light fruit cake, omit the polenta (cornmeal) and use 150 g/5$^{1}/_{2}$ oz/1$^{1}/_{4}$ cups self-raising flour instead.

Chocolate & Almond Torte

This torte is perfect for serving on a hot sunny day with double (heavy) cream and a selection of fresh summer berries.

Serves 10

INGREDIENTS

225 g/8 oz dark chocolate, broken
   into pieces
3 tbsp water
150 g/5^1/$_2$ oz/1 cup soft brown sugar
175 g/6 oz/^{3}/$_4$ cup butter, softened

25 g/1 oz/^{1}/$_4$ cup ground almonds
3 tbsp self-raising flour
5 eggs, separated
100 g 3^1/$_2$ oz/^{1}/$_4$ cup blanched
   almonds, chopped finely

icing (confectioners') sugar, for
   dusting
double (heavy) cream, to serve
   (optional)

1 Grease a 23 cm/9 inch loose-bottomed cake tin (pan) and base line with baking parchment.

2 In a saucepan set over a very low heat, melt the chocolate with the water, stirring until smooth. Add the sugar and stir until dissolved, taking the pan off the heat to prevent it overheating.

3 Add the butter in small amounts until it has melted into the chocolate. Remove from the heat and lightly stir in the ground almonds and flour. Add the egg yolks one at a time, beating well after each addition.

4 In a large mixing bowl, whisk the egg whites until they stand in soft peaks, then fold them into the chocolate mixture with a metal spoon. Stir in the chopped almonds. Pour the mixture into the tin (pan) and level the surface.

5 Bake in a preheated oven, 180°C/350°F/Gas Mark 4, for 40-45 minutes until well risen and firm (the cake will crack on the surface during cooking).

6 Leave the cake to cool in the tin (pan) for 30-40 minutes, then turn it out on to a wire rack to cool completely. Dust with icing (confectioners') sugar and serve in slices with double (heavy) cream, if using.

COOK'S TIP

For a nuttier flavour, toast the chopped almonds in a dry frying pan (skillet) over a medium heat for about 2 minutes until lightly golden.

Carrot Cake

This classic favourite is always popular with children and adults alike when it is served for afternoon tea.

Makes 12 bars

INGREDIENTS

125 g/4^1/2 oz/1 cup self-raising flour
pinch of salt
1 tsp ground cinnamon
125 g/4^1/2 oz/^{3}/4 cup soft brown
  sugar
2 eggs
100 ml/3^1/2 fl oz/scant ^{1}/2 cup
  sunflower oil

125 g/4^1/2 oz carrot, peeled and
  grated finely
25 g/1 oz/^{1}/3 cup desiccated
  (shredded) coconut
25 g/1 oz/^{1}/3 cup walnuts,
  chopped
walnut pieces, for decoration

FROSTING:
50 g/1^3/4 oz/10 tsp butter, softened
50 g/1^3/4 oz full fat soft cheese
225 g/8 oz/1^1/2 cups icing
  (confectioners') sugar, sieved
  (strained)
1 tsp lemon juice

1 Lightly grease a 20 cm/8 inch square cake tin (pan) and line with baking parchment.

2 Sieve (strain) the flour, salt and ground cinnamon into a large bowl and stir in the brown sugar. Add the eggs and oil to the dry ingredients and mix well.

3 Stir in the grated carrot, desiccated (shredded) coconut and chopped walnuts.

4 Pour the mixture into the prepared tin (pan) and bake in a preheated oven, 180°C/350°F/ Gas Mark 4, for 20-25 minutes or until just firm to the touch. Leave to cool in the tin (pan).

5 Meanwhile, make the cheese frosting. In a bowl, beat together the butter, full fat soft cheese, icing (confectioners') sugar and lemon juice until the mixture is fluffy and creamy.

6 Turn the cake out of the tin (pan) and cut into 12 bars or slices. Spread with the frosting and then decorate with walnut pieces.

VARIATION

For a moister cake, replace the coconut with 1 roughly mashed banana.

Coconut Cake

This is a great family favourite. I was always delighted to find it included in my lunch box and considered it a real treat!

Serves 6–8

INGREDIENTS

225 g/8 oz/ self-raising flour (self-rising) flour
pinch of salt
100 g/3¹/₂ oz/¹/₂ cup butter, cut into small pieces

100 g/3¹/₂ oz/¹/₂ cup demerara (brown crystal) sugar
100 g/3¹/₂ oz/1 cup desiccated (shredded) coconut, plus extra for sprinkling

2 eggs, beaten
4 tbsp milk

1 Grease a 900 g/2 lb loaf tin (pan) and line the base with baking parchment.

2 Sieve (strain) the flour and salt into a mixing bowl and rub in the butter with your fingers until the mixture resembles fine breadcrumbs.

3 Stir in the sugar, coconut, eggs and milk and mix to a soft dropping consistency.

4 Spoon the mixture into the prepared tin (pan) and level the surface. Bake in a preheated oven, 160°C/325°F/Gas Mark 3, for 30 minutes.

5 Remove the cake from the oven and sprinkle with the reserved coconut. Return the cake to the oven and cook for a further 30 minutes until well risen and golden and a fine skewer inserted into the centre comes out clean.

6 Leave the cake to cool in the tin (pan) before turning out and transferring to a wire rack to cool completely before serving.

COOK'S TIP

The flavour of this cake is enhanced by storing it in a cool dry place for a few days before eating.

Apple Cake with Cider

This can be eaten as a cake at tea time or with a cup of coffee, or it can be warmed through and served with cream for a dessert.

Makes a 20 cm/8 inch cake

INGREDIENTS

225 g/8 oz/2 cups self-raising flour
1 tsp baking powder
75 g/2³/₄ oz/¹/₃ cup butter, cut into small pieces

75 g/2³/₄ oz/¹/₃ cup caster (superfine) sugar
50 g/1³/₄ oz dried apple, chopped
75 g/2³/₄ oz/5 tbsp raisins

150 ml/¹/₄ pint/²/₃ cup sweet cider
1 egg, beaten
175 g/6 oz raspberries

1 Grease a 20 cm/8 inch cake tin (pan) and line with baking parchment.

2 Sieve (strain) the flour and baking powder into a mixing bowl and rub in the butter with your fingers until the mixture resembles fine breadcrumbs.

3 Stir in the caster (superfine) sugar, chopped dried apple and raisins.

4 Pour in the sweet cider and egg and mix together until thoroughly blended. Stir in the raspberries very gently so they do not break up.

5 Pour the mixture into the prepared cake tin (pan).

6 Bake in a preheated oven, 190°C/375°F/Gas Mark 5, for about 40 minutes until risen and lightly golden.

7 Leave the cake to cool in the tin (pan), then turn out on to a wire rack. Leave until completely cold before serving.

VARIATION

If you don't want to use cider, replace it with clear apple juice, if you prefer.

Coffee & Almond Streusel Cake

*This cake has a moist coffee sponge on the bottom,
covered with a crisp crunchy, spicy topping.*

Serves 8

INGREDIENTS

275 g/9^1/$_2$ oz/1^1/$_4$ cups plain (all-purpose) flour
1 tbsp baking powder
75 g/2^3/$_4$ oz/^{1}/$_3$ cup caster (superfine) sugar
150 ml/^{1}/$_4$ pint/^{2}/$_3$ cup milk
2 eggs
100 g/3^1/$_2$ oz/^{1}/$_2$ cup butter, melted and cooled

2 tbsp instant coffee mixed with 1 tbsp boiling water
50 g/1^3/$_4$ oz/^{1}/$_3$ cup almonds, chopped
icing (confectioners' sugar), for dusting

TOPPING:
75 g/2^3/$_4$ oz/^{1}/$_2$ cup self-raising flour
75 g/2^3/$_4$ oz/^{1}/$_3$ cup demerara (brown crystal) sugar
25 g/1 oz/6 tsp butter, cut into small pieces
1 tsp ground mixed spice (allspice)
1 tbsp water

1 Grease a 23 cm/9 inch loose-bottomed round cake tin (pan) and line with baking parchment. Sieve (strain) together the flour and baking powder into a mixing bowl, then stir in the caster (superfine) sugar.

2 Whisk the milk, eggs, butter and coffee mixture together and pour on to the dry ingredients. Add the chopped almonds and mix lightly together. Spoon the mixture into the tin (pan).

3 To make the topping, mix the flour and demerara (brown crystal) sugar together in a separate bowl.

4 Rub in the butter with your fingers until the mixture is crumbly. Sprinkle in the ground mixed spice (allspice) and the water and bring the mixture together in loose crumbs. Sprinkle the topping over the cake mixture.

5 Bake in a preheated oven, 190°C/375°F/Gas Mark 5, for 50 minutes-1 hour. Cover loosely with foil if the topping starts to brown too quickly. Leave to cool in the tin (pan), then turn out. Dust with icing (confectioners') sugar just before serving.

Gingerbread

*This spicy gingerbread is made even more moist
by the addition of chopped fresh apples.*

Makes 12 bars

INGREDIENTS

150 g/5^1/2 oz/^{2}/3 cup butter
175 g/6 oz/1 cup soft brown sugar
2 tbsp black treacle (molasses)
225 g/8 oz/2 cups plain (all-purpose)
   flour

1 tsp baking powder
2 tsp bicarbonate of soda (baking
   soda)
2 tsp ground ginger
150 ml/^{1}/4 pint/ ^{2}/3 cup milk

1 egg, beaten
2 dessert apples, peeled, chopped and
   coated with 1 tbsp lemon juice

1 Grease a 23 cm/9 inch square cake tin (pan) and line with baking parchment.

2 Melt the butter, sugar and treacle (molasses) in a saucepan over a low heat and leave the mixture to cool.

3 Sieve (strain) the flour, baking powder, bicarbonate of soda (baking soda) and ginger into a mixing bowl.

4 Stir in the milk, beaten egg and cooled buttery liquid, followed by the chopped apples coated with the lemon juice.

5 Mix everything together gently, then pour the mixture into the prepared tin (pan).

6 Bake in a preheated oven, 170°C/325°F/Gas Mark 3, for 30-35 minutes until the cake has risen and a fine skewer inserted into the centre comes out clean.

7 Leave the cake to cool in the tin (pan) before turning out and cutting into 12 bars.

VARIATION

If you enjoy the flavour of ginger, try adding 25 g (1 oz) stem (candied) ginger, chopped finely, to the mixture in step 3.

Cherry Scones

*These are an alternative to traditional scones, using sweet glacé (candied)
cherries which not only create colour but add a distinct flavour.*

Makes 8

INGREDIENTS

225 g/8 oz/2 cups self-raising flour
1 tbsp caster (superfine) sugar
pinch of salt

75 g/2³/4 oz/¹/3 cup butter, cut into
  small pieces
40 g/1¹/2 oz//3 tbsp glacé (candied)
  cherries, chopped

40 g/1¹/2 oz/3 tbsp sultanas (golden
  raisins)
1 egg, beaten
50 ml/2 fl oz/¹/4 cup milk

1 Lightly grease a baking tray (cookie sheet).

2 Sieve (strain) the flour, sugar and salt into a mixing bowl and rub in the butter with your fingers until the scone mixture resembles breadcrumbs.

3 Stir in the glacé (candied) cherries and sultanas (golden raisins). Add the egg.

4 Reserve 1 tablespoon of the milk for glazing, then add the remainder to the mixture. Mix together to form a soft dough.

5 On a lightly floured surface, roll out the dough to a thickness of 2 cm/³/4 inches and cut out 8 scones, using a 5 cm/ 2 inch cutter.

6 Place the scones on to the baking tray (cookie sheet) and brush with the reserved milk.

7 Bake in a preheated oven, 220°C/425°F/Gas Mark 7, for 8-10 minutes or until the scones are golden brown.

8 Leave to cool on a wire rack, then serve split and buttered.

COOK'S TIP

*These scones will freeze very
successfully but they are best
defrosted and eaten within
1 month.*

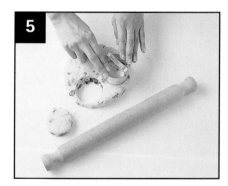

Cranberry Muffins

*These savoury muffins are an ideal accompaniment to soup, or
they make a nice change from sweet cakes for serving with coffee.*

Makes 18

INGREDIENTS

225 g/8 oz/2 cups plain (all-purpose) flour
2 tsp baking powder
$^1/_2$ tsp salt

50 g/1$^3/_4$ oz/9 tsp caster (superfine) sugar
50 g/1$^3/_4$ oz/10 tsp butter, melted
2 eggs, beaten

200 ml/7 fl oz/$^3/_4$ cup milk
100 g/3$^1/_2$ oz fresh cranberries
2 tbsp freshly grated Parmesan cheese

1 Lightly grease 2 bun (patty) tins (pans).

2 Sieve (strain) the flour, baking powder and salt into a mixing bowl. Stir in the caster (superfine) sugar.

3 In a separate bowl, mix the butter, beaten eggs and milk together, then pour into the bowl of dry ingredients.

4 Mix lightly together until all of the ingredients are evenly combined, then stir in the fresh cranberries.

5 Divide the mixture between the prepared tins (pans).

6 Sprinkle the grated Parmesan cheese over the top of each muffin mixture.

7 Bake in a preheated oven, 200°C/400°F/Gas Mark 6, for about 20 minutes or until the muffins are well risen and a golden brown colour.

8 Leave the muffins to cool in the tins (pans). Transfer the muffins to a wire rack and leave to cool completely before serving.

VARIATION

For a sweet alternative to this recipe, replace the Parmesan cheese with demerara (brown crystal) sugar in step 6, if you prefer.

Spiced Biscuits (Cookies)

These spicy biscuits (cookies) are perfect to serve with fruit salad or ice cream for a very easy instant dessert.

Makes about 24

INGREDIENTS

175 g/6 oz/^{3}/$_4$ cup unsalted butter
175 g/6 oz/1 cup dark muscovado sugar
225 g/8 oz/2 cups plain (all-purpose) flour

pinch of salt
^{1}/$_2$ tsp bicarbonate of soda (baking soda)
1 tsp ground cinnamon
^{1}/$_2$ tsp ground coriander

^{1}/$_2$ tsp ground nutmeg
^{1}/$_4$ tsp ground cloves
2 tbsp dark rum

1 Lightly grease 2 baking trays (cookie sheets).

2 Cream together the butter and sugar and whisk until light and fluffy.

3 Sieve (strain) the flour, salt, bicarbonate of soda (baking soda), cinnamon, coriander, nutmeg and cloves into the creamed mixture.

4 Stir the dark rum into the creamed mixture.

5 Using 2 teaspoons, place small mounds of the mixture, on to the baking trays (cookie sheets), placing them 7 cm/3 inch apart to allow for spreading during cooking. Flatten each one slightly with the back of a spoon.

6 Bake in a preheated oven, 180°C/350°F/Gas Mark 4, for 10-12 minutes until golden.

7 Leave the biscuits (cookies) to cool and crispen on wire racks before serving.

COOK'S TIP

Use the back of a fork to flatten the biscuits (cookies) slightly before baking.

Gingernuts

Nothing compares to the taste of these freshly baked authentic gingernuts which have a lovely hint of orange flavour.

Makes 30

INGREDIENTS

350 g/12 oz/3 cups self-raising (self-rising) flour
pinch of salt
200 g/7 oz/1 cup caster (superfine) sugar

1 tbsp ground ginger
1 tsp bicarbonate of soda (baking soda)
125 g/4^1/$_2$ oz/^{1}/$_2$ cup butter

75 g/2^3/$_4$ oz/^{1}/$_4$ cup golden (light corn) syrup
1 egg, beaten
1 tsp grated orange rind

1 Lightly grease several baking trays (cookie sheets).

2 Sieve (strain) the flour, salt, sugar, ginger and bicarbonate of soda (baking soda) into a large mixing bowl.

3 Heat the butter and golden (light corn) syrup together in a saucepan over a very low heat until the butter has melted.

4 Leave the butter mixture to cool slightly, then pour it on to the dry ingredients.

5 Add the egg and orange rind and mix thoroughly.

6 Using your hands, carefully shape the dough into 30 even-sized balls.

7 Place the balls well apart on the prepared baking trays (cookie sheets), then flatten them slightly with your fingers.

8 Bake in a preheated oven, 160°C/325°F/Gas Mark 3, for 15-20 minutes, then transfer them to a wire rack to cool.

COOK'S TIP

Store these biscuits in an airtight container and eat them within 1 week.

VARIATION

If you like your gingernuts crunchy, bake them in the oven for a few minutes longer.

Oat & Raisin Biscuits (Cookies)

These oaty, fruity biscuits (cookies) are delicious with a cup of tea!

Makes 10

INGREDIENTS

50 g/1³/₄ oz/10 tsp butter
125 g/4¹/₂ oz/¹/₂ cup caster
   (superfine) sugar
1 egg, beaten

50 g/1³/₄/¹/₂ cup plain (all-purpose)
   flour
¹/₂ tsp salt
¹/₂ tsp baking powder

175 g/6 oz/2 cups porridge oats
125 g/4¹/₂ oz/³/₄ cup raisins
2 tbsp sesame seeds

1 Lightly grease 2 baking trays (cookie sheets).

2 In a large mixing bowl, cream together the butter and sugar until light and fluffy.

3 Add the beaten egg gradually and beat until well combined.

4 Sieve (strain) the flour, salt and baking powder into the creamed mixture. Mix well.

5 Add the porridge oats, raisins and sesame seeds and mix together thoroughly.

6 Place spoonfuls of the mixture well apart on the prepared baking trays (cookie sheets) and flatten them slightly with the back of a spoon.

7 Bake in a preheated oven, 180°C/350°F/Gas Mark 4, for 15 minutes.

8 Leave the biscuits (cookies) to cool slightly on the baking trays (cookie sheets).

9 Transfer the biscuits (cookies) to a wire rack and leave to cool completely before serving.

VARIATION

Substitute chopped ready-to-eat dried apricots for the raisins, if you prefer.

COOK'S TIP

To enjoy these biscuits (cookies) at their best, store them in an airtight container.

Millionaire's Shortbread

These rich squares of shortbread are topped with caramel and finished with chocolate to make a very special treat!

Makes 12 bars

INGREDIENTS

175 g/6 oz/1¹/₂ cups plain (all-purpose) flour

125 g/4¹/₂ oz/¹/₂ cup butter, cut into small pieces

50 g/1³/₄ oz/3 tbsp soft brown sugar, sieved (strained)

TOPPING:

50 g/1³/₄ oz/10 tsp butter

50 g/1³/₄ oz/3 tbsp soft brown sugar

400 g/14 oz can condensed milk

150 g/5¹/₂ oz milk chocolate

1 Grease a 23 cm/9 inch square cake tin (pan).

2 Sieve (strain) the flour into a mixing bowl and rub in the butter with your fingers until the mixture resembles fine breadcrumbs. Add the sugar and mix to form a firm dough.

3 Press the dough into the bottom of the prepared tin (pan) and prick with a fork.

4 Bake in a preheated oven, 190°C/375°F/Gas Mark 5, for 20 minutes until lightly golden. Leave to cool in the tin (pan).

5 To make the topping, place the butter, sugar and condensed milk in a non-stick saucepan and cook over a gentle heat, stirring constantly, until the mixture comes to the boil.

6 Reduce the heat and cook for 4-5 minutes until the caramel is pale golden and thick and is coming away from the sides of the pan. Pour the topping over the shortbread base and leave to cool.

7 When the caramel topping is firm, melt the milk chocolate in a heatproof bowl set over a saucepan of simmering water. Spread the melted chocolate over the topping, leave to set in a cool place, then cut the shortbread into squares or fingers to serve.

COOK'S TIP

Ensure the caramel layer is completely cool and set before coating it with the melted chocolate, otherwise they will mix together.

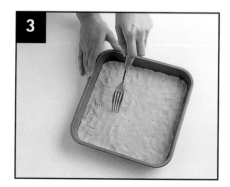

Rock Drops

These rock drops are more substantial than a crisp biscuit (cookie).
Serve them fresh from the oven to enjoy them at their best.

Makes 8

INGREDIENTS

200 g/7 oz/1¾ cups plain (all-purpose) flour
2 tsp baking powder
100 g/3½ oz/⅓ cup butter, cut into small pieces

75 g/2¾ oz/⅓ cup demerara (brown crystal) sugar
100 g/3½ oz/½ cup sultanas (golden raisins)

25 g/1 oz/2 tbsp glacé (candied) cherries, chopped finely
1 egg, beaten
2 tbsp milk

1 Lightly grease a baking tray (cookie sheet).

2 Sieve (strain) the flour and baking powder into a mixing bowl. Rub in the butter with your fingers until the mixture resembles breadcrumbs.

3 Stir in the sugar, sultanas (golden raisins) and chopped glacé (candied) cherries.

4 Add the beaten egg and the milk to the mixture and mix to form a soft dough.

5 Spoon 8 mounds of the mixture on to the baking tray (cookie sheet), spacing them well apart as they will spread while they are cooking.

6 Bake in a preheated oven, 200°C/400°F/Gas Mark 6, for 15-20 minutes until firm to the touch when pressed with a finger.

7 Remove the rock drops from the baking tray (cookie sheet). Either serve piping hot from the oven or transfer to a wire rack and leave to cool before serving.

COOK'S TIP

For convenience, prepare the dry ingredients in advance and just before cooking stir in the liquid.

Chocolate Chip Brownies

*Choose a good quality chocolate for these chocolate chip brownies
to give them a rich flavour that is not too sweet.*

Makes 12

INGREDIENTS

150 g/5^1/2 oz dark chocolate, broken
 into pieces
225 g/8 oz/1 cup butter, softened
225 g/8 oz/2 cups self-raising flour

125 g/4^1/2 oz/^{1}/2 cup caster
 (superfine) sugar
4 eggs, beaten
75 g/2^3/4 oz pistachio nuts,
 chopped

100 g/3^1/2 oz white chocolate,
 chopped roughly
icing (confectioners') sugar, for
 dusting

1 Lightly grease a 23 cm/9 inch baking tin (pan) and line with greaseproof paper.

2 Melt the dark chocolate and butter in a heatproof bowl set over a saucepan of simmering water. Leave to cool slightly.

3 Sieve (strain) the flour into a separate mixing bowl and stir in the caster (superfine) sugar.

4 Stir the eggs into the melted chocolate mixture, then pour this mixture into the flour and sugar mixture, beating well. Stir in the pistachio nuts and white chocolate, then pour the mixture into the tin (pan), spreading it evenly into the corners.

5 Bake in a preheated oven, 180°C/350°/Gas Mark 4, for 30-35 minutes until firm to the touch. Leave to cool in the tin (pan) for 20 minutes, then turn out on to a wire rack.

6 Dust the brownie with icing (confectioners') sugar and cut into 12 pieces when cold.

COOK'S TIP

The brownie won't be completely firm in the middle when it is removed from the oven, but it will set when it has cooled.

Florentines

These luxury biscuits (cookies) will be popular at any time of the year but make a wonderful treat for Christmas-time.

Makes 8–10

INGREDIENTS

50 g/1³/₄ oz/ 10 tsp butter
50 g/1³/₄ oz/¹/₄ cup caster (superfine) sugar
25 g/1 oz/¹/₄ cup plain (all-purpose) flour, sieved (strained)

50 g/1³/₄ oz/¹/₃ cup almonds, chopped
50 g/1³/₄ oz/¹/₃ cup chopped mixed peel
25 g/1 oz/¹/₄ cup raisins, chopped

25 g/1 oz/2 tbsp glacé (candied) cherries, chopped
finely grated rind of ¹/₂ lemon
125 g/4¹/₂ oz dark chocolate, melted

1 Line 2 large baking trays (cookie sheets) with baking parchment.

2 Heat the butter and caster (superfine) sugar in a small saucepan until the butter has just melted and the sugar dissolved. Remove the pan from the heat.

3 Stir in the flour and mix well. Stir in the chopped almonds, mixed peel, raisins, cherries and lemon rind. Place teaspoonfuls of the mixture well apart on the baking trays (cookie sheets).

4 Bake in a preheated oven, 180°C/350°F/Gas Mark 4, for 10 minutes or until lightly golden.

5 As soon as the florentines are removed from the oven, press the edges into neat shapes while still on the baking trays (cookie sheets), using a biscuit (cookie) cutter. Leave to cool on the baking trays (cookie sheets) until firm, then transfer to a wire rack to cool completely.

6 Spread the melted chocolate over the smooth side of each florentine. As the chocolate begins to set, mark wavy lines in it with a fork. Leave the florentines until set, chocolate side up.

VARIATION

Replace the dark chocolate with white chocolate or, for a dramatic effect, cover half of the florentines in dark chocolate and half in white.

This is a Parragon Publishing Book
First published in 2003

Parragon Publishing
Queen Street House
4 Queen Street, Bath, BA1 1HE, UK

All recipes and photography compiled from material
created by 'Haldane Mason', and 'The Foundry'.

Cover design by Shelley Doyle.

ISBN: 1-40540-839-1

Printed in China

NOTE

Cup measurements in this book are for American cups. This book uses
imperial and metric measurements. Follow the same units of measurement
throughout; do not mix imperial and metric. All spoon measurements are
level; teaspoons are assumed to be 5 ml and tablespoons are assumed to be
15 ml. Unless otherwise stated, milk is assumed to be whole milk, eggs
and individual vegetables such as potatoes are medium, and pepper is
freshly ground black pepper.

The times given for each recipe are an approximate guide only because
the preparation times may differ according to the techniques used by
different people and the cooking times may vary as a result of the
type of oven used.

Recipes using raw or very lightly cooked eggs should be avoided by
infants, the elderly, pregnant women, convalescents and anyone
suffering from an illness.